Cover Page

THINK
YOU CAN

Your Imaginative Power, Is Your Creative Ability

Ivan Mawanda

(First Edition)

For information, please contact the publisher: IVAN MAWANDA
www.ivanmawanda.com

Email: mawanda351@gmail.com,
Cell: +256752942434

Available online on Amazon Kindle Bookstore

Type(s): Educative / Godly / Motivational novel

ISBN: 978-9970-9621-0-5

Layout: Joseph Kevin Kulubya
Design: Nabukwasi Brenda
Cover Photo: Kawooya John & Mick Ruiz

Editorial Assistance: Regina Asinde
Editorial Consultant: Pamella Magino
Printed and bound in Uganda by Elite Graphics Ltd

CD/2021/46

NCDC
NATIONAL CURRICULUM
DEVELOPMENT CENTRE

Certificate of Approval

This is to certify that this material:
"THINK YOU CAN"

By: IVAN MAWANDA.

has been evaluated by National Curriculum
Development Centre and deemed
appropriate for use at All Levels.
(General Purpose Reader)

Signed
DIRECTOR
NCDC

Dedication

In life we don't meet by accident. They are diligently meant to cross our paths for a reason.

Through prayers, I dedicate this book to every reader who feels inferiority complex... Sorry, Life is like that sometimes but the only secret to success is that think fruitfully, with hard work but not unfortunate speculations. Think You Can emphasis is best constructive to learners from 12years to young adults however reading this book may never be limited to any age if we are to transform our society.

Remember not all opportunities are taken; some are set as a trap; did you know that a person can become so determined to destroy you that they may become blind and end up destroying themselves.

Acknowledgements

It is a genuine pleasure to express deep gratitude to my

mentors, Biyi Bandele in London (UK), Phad Rhymz Mutumba in Quebec (Canada) and Lukas Kosztolanyi in Dublin – Ireland, Prof. Wole Soyinka, The Boys and Girls Brigade (1st Mengo company – St. Paul's Cathedral, Namirembe). Their overwhelming advice, dedication and keen interest in helping me develop my talent has made me who I am today. They have been solely responsible for the completion of this work.

I owe a deep sense of gratitude to Senior Counsel Mutyaba Vincent (R.I.P), for his keen interest in me at the initial stage of developing my talent. His prompt inspirations, timely suggestions and dynamism have enabled me during my pursuit.

I would also profusely like to thank Bigsam carstine kisakye, Dr. Lina Zedriga (PhD), Hon. Charles Batambuze (ASSHU & URRO), Counsel Peter Mugimba, writers and organizations that guided me through different stages to the

completion of this book. I greatly appreciate your help, encouragement, co-operation and above all your support.

Last but not least, I want to thank my family, who supported and encouraged me inspite of all the time it took.

Above all I wish to thank the Almighty God. Without Him, I would not have managed to get this book to this stage.

Contents

Foreword

Ssaabasajja Kabaka Awangaale
Oweek. Dr. Nakindu Prosperous Kavuma (PhD)
Minister For Social Services In Charge of Health,
Education, Women and Gender.
Nnaabagereka's Office, Buganda Kingdom

I thank you Mawanda Ivan for giving me the opportunity to write a foreword to your Educational and Inspirational book "Think You Can". Thinking is one of the skills which are not common but very necessary in the 21st century. Actually, according to Griffin. P. (2014), one of the 21st century skills is critical thinking. This means if one can't think, can't set his mind in motion, that person will miss the core of the century.

This book shows the power of thinking. The power of thinking is an alternative system for outlining information that is hierarchical in nature. Further, positive thinking is a mental and emotional attitude that focuses on the bright side of life and expects positive results.

A person with positive thinking anticipates happiness, health and success, and believes that he or she can overcome any obstacle and difficulty. The author of this book, Mawanda Ivan gave it a title "Think You Can" this title is very inspirational. It indicates positivity of mind. If you are determined as the author teaches us in chapter 4, you are most likely to win and the reverse is true other attributes like personality, knowledge, focus and choice are secondary.

As you read this book, I argue you to enjoy the experience shared and the content here in. I once again appreciate the author who has not only told us about his dreams but has shown us through writing this book amidst a lot of challenges.

Harvard Law School, USA
Prof. Lina Zedriga Waru (PhD)
Director/Lecturer
Women, Peace and Security

'NOTHING ABOUT US WITHOUT US' has been invoked by many to inspire the need to take action for transformational leadership in social movements within society at any level. Ivan Mawanda has dared to say that we all have the power to think and shape our future, challenge our present and demystify our past through thinking in practice. He invokes the need for setting standards in practice through personal attributes of imploring that ability to be human and asks each one of us to say **"NOTHING ABOUT ME WITHOUT ME'**. In many situations and encounters I come across sayings like **WE NEED INCLUSION**, we are excluded from decision making, we are not participating but Ivan has reshaped all this.

In a world where personal accountability, innovation, and critical decisions have been turned into what often degenerates depression, self-pity, blame game by many who experience situations of physical need, poverty, scarcity resulting them into struggling to survive. Ivan's writing demystifies this notion. Rather it provokes, inspires, beckons, challenges and leads each one of us to think in practice, to think of solutions, alternatives and never resign to fate. This book unveils an inner reality of the power of thinking positively, of holding onto and trusting in your attitude and power to un-look, of the continuous calls to have a positive attitude. It constantly reminded me of the saying that 'Life is what you make it

It can and have been broken, for that reason we are what we think'

At this young and tender age, coming from a very challenging background in an environment so uncertain where many young people have drifted and sentenced themselves to failures, self-pitty, negative peer influence. Ivan has dared and shown in practice that Success is very possible; it does not matter where each one of us is coming from. He invokes the popular call to action, the popular sayings that 'Be the Change you want to see', the Biblical saying that we are all made in the Image of God, we all matter and are equal before the Lord God Almighty, as it is clearly stated in the 1995 Republic of Uganda Constitution under Constitutional Provision of Article 21 that All person are Equal before and under the law. And does it in a very practical, everyday experience of human beings that you will find so easy to relate and refer to.

This book will challenge you not only to read and re-read but take your pen or your computer, to start writing your story, to start waking up from slumber/ early resignation by giving up and tell your story. Ivan inspires us not to resign to destiny but rather reclaim our dignity and create a platform to speak, to be heard.
It is a book not to gather dust in our book shelves but be a companion every day. It is a worthwhile reference, very compelling piece for all and indeed a standard apart.

A timely book for our times and those yet to come which I very highly recommend to all persons male and female, young and old, creed, or social, economic and whatever standing. It speaks out very loud in ways you have never experienced. If this book was a song, it would have been and I dare say it is a hit. Thanks you so much Ivan, I can't await to see your next inspirational book title.

Cambridge University, UK
Dr. Drake Sekeeba(PhD)
Mass Communication

This is great work, factual and enterprising with originality to mentor everyone by self-analysis, self-education which improves their ability to make decisions. Ivan Mawanda is a true mentor based on the message conveyed in this book which I highly recommend to everyone. Let us learn these principles and apply them in our daily life; it's the only way to get the most out of it if you want to get a real lasting benefit out of here!

Prof. Peter Waswa (PhD)
Makerere University

I truly agree with Ivan Mawanda, this book has real concepts in the journey to greatness through thinking; I once shared this concept with students on their graduation day at Makerere University.

"Academic excellence is overrated!
I said it. Being top of your class does not necessarily guarantee that they will be at the top in life. You could be the best student in finance, but it doesn't mean you will make more than everyone else. The best graduating Law student does not necessarily become the best lawyer. The fact is life requires more than the ability to understand a concept, then after memorise it and reproduce it in an exam. Any school may reward an excellent student for his or her memory, but life rewards on individual merit anyone for his or her imagination. School rewards caution, life rewards daring. School hails those who live by the rules. Life exalts those who break the rules and set new ones. So do I mean people should not study hard in school?

Oh, no, you should. But do not sacrifice every other thing on the altar of first class. Do not limit yourself to the classroom. Do something practical. Take a leadership position. Start a business and fail. That's a better Entrepreneurship skill. Join or start a club. Contest an election and lose. It will teach you something Political Science will not teach you. Attend a seminar. Read books outside the scope of your course. Go on missions and win a soul for eternal rewards... do something you be lieve in! Think less of becoming an excellent student but think more of becoming an excellent person. Do not make the classroom to be your world but make your classroom. Step forward and try politics, try business, try farming, try an extra thing..."

Dantes Kashangire
National Secretary,
The Boys and Girls Brigade
(Uganda)

I recall and do appreciate Ivan Mawanda once a boy member in the Boys Brigade of Uganda – First Mengo company for his time well used to reflect back to his journey of growth from childhood to date, then he came up with this inspiring book titled, "Think You Can." I believe and hope that you too will be inspired by his thoughts, ask yourself what mistakes you have made and what improvement or lessons you learned for the future? This nature of a book compilation was his original idea, by which he shares with pleasure his journey of growth experience. He critically outlines how he made it in developing his talents at different levels up the present day.

To him as an author, looking at his experiences over the years and the environment around him seemingly compelled him to write this book "Think You Can." So that the present and future generation can read, understand and comprehend for pleasure but in the long run get motivated to always think positively about their life.

In his thinking, he analyzed life to be strange...though appearing in different format that's according to how each one views it. He challenges all the readers that anything can be impossible to achieve if we tend not to think positively.

Lastly, "Think You Can" can be a very transforming book; it can change us for better and lead us to discover our potential. Be grateful to Ivan Mawanda as I am.

Phillip .M. Baitwa
League of young professional,
Director
Kampala-Uganda

The book **THINK YOU CAN** has come timely to address the generational challenge of a poor attitude. As a young man, one of the best decisions I have taken in my life was the day I decided to work on my mindset and attitude to turn my life around. I have seen the author struggle as a young man to keep positive despite the challenges and storms he met in putting this great material together but I have also seen how the power beyond imagination has kept him aggressive, creative, positive and changed to finally enjoy the fruits of his patience and attitude.

This life we live in is product of our thinking, our words, our actions and results. I have taken off time to read and appreciate the book **THINK YOU CAN** and I have found it to be rich in shaping perspectives about the daily life we live and the daily thoughts that run this life. When I was young, I used to admire riding a bicycle and I would want to ride every guest's bicycle that came home and my parents did not like this since as a child I would spoil guest's bicycles all the time. I often failed several times to balance the bicycle which made me fall down, sustaining several injuries on my legs and arms. To make it worse, I was beaten by my Dad several times but stubbornly this wasn't a limitation for me to pick up the bicycle until I balanced it with no one holding or supporting me. This is what they call the character of thinking you can, no matter what comes your way.

The author who happens to be among the people I mentor came to office and was bounced several times intentionally or by coincidence to check whether he had the **THINK YOU CAN** attitude, but I must say he passed the test with a distinction...by never getting tired to return and send emails for what he wanted. There is nothing as powerful as a made up mind whose focus is never to quit until it achieves the intended results and that's the real experience you will learn from this book.

Every little child learning to stand or walk never gets tired of falling down because the attitude window is clean with an innocent **THINK YOU CAN** character. I encourage all young people to pick a copy of this book for friends, family and workmates to help break their barriers in thinking, acting and in the end get excellent results.

The book will trigger your mind to think more about the life you live and how possible you see yourself achieve your dreams. Think you can and you will achieve people in your life who will cheer you up and lift up your spirit.

Think you can and every difficulty and challenge will be broken through with ease because of a great force of a determined mind.

My thinking right now is that you can.

Edton Babu Batwana
Project Director AYEDI,
World Education
Kampala, Uganda

Ivan Mawanda is a very inspiring, God fearing, and down to earth Person. He has used his personal experience to inspire readers towards greatness in this book Think You Can. The Power of the mind cannot be underestimated because you are what you think you are. Ivan has been able to weave in key lessons on working toward greatness beginning by working on your mind. His personal life encounters have created rich fodder for him to practically bring out the subject matter of this book. It is my sincere belief that the readers of this book will be greatly blessed and we embark on the journey to greatness through perfecting our thoughts.

Jackie Lumbasi
Capital Radio/UBC

I thank Ivan Mawanda for this inspirational book titled Think You Can. I am emphasizing to anyone who is looking for the core principles of transformation from a negative attitude to positivity towards life. Someone might be stuck in a life situation that seems difficult to carry on; however this book is an eye opener to the fact that tears may flow for some time but not all the time...it's not yet over and nothing is impossible.

Age-wise 13years can read and understand every chapter relating to real life. At times anyone of any age may get evil imaginations from self-pity, frustration, oppression, rejection, brutality, bitterness, depression or traumatic stress disorder then ends up complaining and murmuring; I believe "Think You Can" is the best solution!

Why This Book Was Written?

No one stops you to think even though it seems like it is the hardest work, that's why very few engage in it. No dream is too big, no challenge is too great, and nothing we want for our future is beyond our reach. By thinking, I mean that you stop what you are doing, concentrate on the subject or problem that must be solved and force yourself to come up with a new idea or solution.

I am greatly irritated by some people who have a mantra: "Life is hard". Often when I hear them say this, I am tempted to ask, "Compared to what?" As the cliche goes, life is what you make it. If you think it's hard, it is hard. If you think it's easy, it will be easy. It all begins and ends with your thinking. Everything is possible; your-dreams, your ideas, your inventions, your visions. Never let anyone tell you that you can't. Think you can and it will be.

Beloved, this book Think you can emphasizes your progress beyond imagination, aggressive but dignified yet frank-filled in nature. This is a noble tool to build and encourage the voice of reason with every opportunity that avails itself so that you can have an excellent tale ending. Read keenly every chapter then you'll humbly understand when or how to seek knowledge and integrate it with your choices.

This will make you assess life in a constructive way. Think you can or think you can't; either way you're right.
We are what we repeatedly do; excellence is therefore not an act but a habit. Never be bullied into silence, never allow yourself to be made a victim; never accept one's

definition of your life, define yourself. "You can't stop people from talking about you; but you can stop giving them what to talk about", and the worst thing to being blind is to have sight with no vision.

Make it your ambition to live a quiet life, to mind your own business and work with your own hands. Have a positive mindset,
Learn how to handle fear. It is never too late to start so don't give up no matter how hard it gets, you have what it takes to be successful? Just go for it and make a difference.

My life experience sometime back when I communicated to some people that I wanted to write this book, not all but some asked me, "Ivan... Why are you so ambitious? Hmmm... and the challenge is you don't listen, have you any idea how difficult it is?"

Guess why?

To cut the long story short, I silently ignored their critics and kept my cards for myself inclined to work harder since these friends were misleading me with a bad attitude or faulty thinking. I knew none of them was God to predict my ability. All learning begins with a simple phrase, "I don't know" but some people believe they completed learning the moment they stepped out of school. How mistaken they are?

Without imagining that each person was given the brain to think, we must be good stewards with them and consciously think more every day..."Brain storming". No matter how you run, you still have yourself to deal with; this could be circumstances or in the mindset. The single most important decision in your life other than regretting is to read this factual inspirational book, with God all things are possible...then happiness will be 100% your responsibility.

PART ONE:
SEEK KNOWDLEGE

Seek Wisdom & Knowledge

I don't pretend to be older than my granny; but the deep truth is despite my 26 years of age, I'm old enough to confess that thoughts are the building blocks of life. Your ability to think, plan, and work hard in the short term is the key to discipline yourself to do what is right and necessary towards creating a wonderful future for yourself before you do what is fun and easy. The ability to think long term is a developed skill. As you get better at it, you become more able to predict with increasing accuracy what is likely to happen to you in the future as the result of your actions. This is a quality of the superior thinker!

Longfellow once wrote, "Those heights by great men, won and kept, were not achieved by sudden flight. But, while their companions slept, they were toiling upward in the night."

In deeper context it's expound as Self-esteem...the opinion you have for your own self! If you feel you're competent and kind, good looking, or capable of doing good things, this is a sign of high self-esteem. But, if you have negative opinions about yourself and feel that you cannot do your tasks like others do or do not look good, you have low self-esteem. Sometimes, low self-esteem becomes the cause of anxiety and depression. Therefore, self-esteem refers to how you think about your own self, how worthy you think you are and how much importance you give to yourself, but knowing that you can do your best, even if you're not perfect.

The year was 1990 when my elder sister Justine graduated from Shimon Teacher's college. She began her career as our Sunday school teacher at Church of Uganda while privately teaching me all the junior school subjects whenever she got back home since I could not afford school fees. With time in 1993, my elder sister Justine was recruited by Kasubi Parents School and the school Director, Forence Senkungu, was kind enough to register me at the age of 5 years in Grade 1 as a needy orphan to study with children from wealthy families. To me it was a miracle and I thanked God for that!

By the time I made 10 years old in Grade 5, that's when my sister talked to me about Seeking Knowledge. Deep inside me, I was too inquisitive to know whether it related to the school subjects I learnt or the games I played while at school. The environment was strange, but every day in a slow and soft voice after classes she'd repeatedly tell me, "Ivan... read hard so that you get good grades, seek knowledge and wisdom. That's the only way you'll progress in life. That pen is mightier than any weapon, open the doors of your mind with books, consider books as your best friend."

Deep inside me I'd question myself; "Seek knowledge and wisdom?" Does this mean I must often use the library, lead in class tests and exams or associate with informed people? " Ok, I'll read hard.

Reasoning as a young boy I had to turn my positive mindset into action and relate it to my purpose or reason. I wasn't muscular in nature that's why all my concentration had to get diverted into academics rather than sports. On the sports day event, only skilled and vigorous students had to represent their school-teams.

However when it got to the end of term academic results, the champions in sports had the vice-versa with academics. I would lead them with flying colors. The school director always offered me more presents at the end of year parent's day. To my surprise she referred to me as, "Ivan... the intellectual and genius."

With all the excitement and joy after having been promoted to Grade 6 due to my great performance, I visited Aunt Florence, the school director with two concerns on my mind. First was to thank her for her kindness and support towards my education and secondly make it a point to inquire from her about knowledge. The latter was too serious during school times but surprisingly, she would warmly welcome me to her living room most especially during holidays to interact. Indirectly, she was parenting me to widen my understanding according to different situations.

"Define for me knowledge and wisdom?" I asked her. "Ooh... why you are curious to know about this Ivan?" she asked after I posed my question.

In a puzzled look, I responded, "Because you mention me as the best student in class, intelligent and genius but not wise or knowledgeable.

She ordered her maid to call other family members; Teddy, Robert, Junior and Fiona. Hey switch off the T.V, as soon as they arrived, she began to expound, "Knowledge is the fact of knowing about something or awareness of a particular skill or situation with intellectual understanding, but the currency that purchases the future is wisdom with which we use what we have. Wisdom is proved right by actions, it can be seen not just heard and it's always justified by its product, not its voice." Which made me raise up my hand to ask, "Is it true that the fear of the lord is the beginning of wisdom as we are taught at Sunday school?"

Aunt Florence pulled her glasses to the bridge of her nose, which truly meant... "Wow, you got it right boy and that's why I like you." She ordered her maid to prepare us some tea and snacks because the conversation was getting extra ordinary.

In her detailed explanation, she told us that if you seek knowledge wisely, it automatically adopts your intelligent ability to be a creative thinker; which enables you to plan efficiently. Finally, to focus on friends who are continuously moving towards excellence in every aspect of their lives, feed yourselves with knowledge and information which may guide you to understand how worth being intelligent is? But wisdom achieves better results:

1. Intelligence leads to arguments. Wisdom leads to settlements.

2. Intelligence is power of will. Wisdom is power over will.

3. Intelligence is heat, it burns. Wisdom is warmth, it comforts.

4. Intelligence is pursuit of knowledge, it tires the seeker. Wisdom is pursuit of truth, it inspires the seeker.

5. Intelligence is holding on. Wisdom is letting go.

6. Intelligence leads you. Wisdom guides you.

7. An intelligent person thinks he knows everything. A wise person knows that there is still something to learn.

8. An intelligent person always tries to prove his point. A wise person knows there really is no point.

9. An intelligent person freely gives unsolicited advice. A wise person keeps his counsel until all options are considered.

10. An intelligent person understands what is being said. A wise person understands what is left unsaid.

11. An intelligent person speaks when he has to say something. A wise person speaks when he has something to say.

12. An intelligent person sees everything as relative. A wise person sees everything as related.

My sister came in through the pouch with conscious curiosity as I rolled my chair back against the wall. She said, "Ivan, you shouldn't delay till 6:00pm because of watching T.V, remember you have to bath." But Aunt Florence politely answered her, "They are here for an important lesson which will impact their life and it's about how they should seek knowledge. I had to have reasonable time with them rather than doing it in a classroom style." She was a kind and patient lady who always narrated her profile. She told us that she graduated with a Bachelor's Degree in Education at Makerere University, then Post Graduated Diploma in Human Resource at Makerere University Business School and pursued a Certificate in Business Management at Management Training and Advisory Centre. We were all mesmerized by the academic achievements she had made. We all asked in disbelief, "All this into one head?" She laughed and said, "Yes." She added that she couldn't manage this school without all the relevant skills. Shocked, we asked, "So that meant we have a long way to go?"

"Absolutely", she replied. "In every aspect of life before being informed and transformed with knowledge from all the different avenues through which you can access it, what you need initially is learning to focus your mind on what results you want to achieve. What do you want to achieve through learning? What kinds of knowledge are you pursuing and why? If you don't know why you want to learn, then distractions will be far more enticing," she added. She told us that when one wisely seeks knowledge, it automatically adopts your intelligent ability to be a creative thinker; and also enables you to solve problems and evaluate their repercussions or consequences while planning efficiently. A wise person usually knows the right thing to do or does what he/she knows.

"Another popular explanation is that wisdom comes from experience while intelligence is innate, but people are not simply wise in proportion to how much experience they have. You'll never find a wise person who is idle or lazy after all it is the diligent that stand before kings. If you diligently use wisdom you will receive a crown at the end." She then asked, "Did you know that wise people can even learn from someone who is mad?" In other words learning is a continuous process.

I, for one, know that the pursuit of knowledge is not a piece of cake or as some people say it is not a matter of eating bananas and beef. It is a daunting task to learn new things. However, it can be done. My perception is if one person can learn something, so can you which means every skill is learned; With the exception of bodily functions. Persist.

Don't give up learning in the face of intimidating tasks. Anything one human being can learn, you too can learn. Wasn't it Einstein who said, "Genius is 1% inspiration and 99% perspiration?"

Thomas Edison said it, too. It may take you more effort, but if you set a believable goal, it will most likely turn into an achievable goal. Be principled. Sir W. Clement Stone once said, "Whatever the mind of man can conceive, it can achieve." It's an amazing phenomenon in goal achievement. Prepare yourself by whatever means necessary, and hurdles will seem surmountable. Anyone who has experienced this phenomenon understands its validity. There's no point in setting learning goals for yourself if you don't have any faith in your ability to learn. Life-changing knowledge does typically require advanced learning techniques. In fact, it's been said that the average adult only uses 10% of his/her brain.

Learn complex problem solving and critical thinking. For most people, life is a series of problems to be solved. Learning is part of the process. If you have a complex problem, you need to learn the art of complex problems. Collaborate. If studying or teaching yourself isn't working, maybe studying in a group will help.

Do unto others: teach something. The best way to learn something better is to teach it to someone else. It forces you to learn, if you are motivated enough to share your knowledge!

Learn the right things first. Learn the basics. Case in point: a frustrating way to learn a new language is to learn grammar and spelling and sentence constructs first.
This is not the way a baby learns a language, and there's no reason why an adult or young adult has to start differently, despite "expert" opinion. Try for yourself and see the difference.

Plan your learning. If you have a long-term plan to learn something, then to quote Led Zeppelin, *"There are two paths you can go by."* You can take a haphazard approach to learning, or you can put in a bit of planning and find an optimum path. Plan your time and balance your learning and living.

Find experts in the field. Ask questions and more questions. Take courses and ask your teacher questions. Don't just sit there. As you begin a new subject or reach a new plateau in your studies, there may be awkward and embarrassing moments. Don't be afraid or think that you lack the aptitude to succeed. Everyone goes through the same learning curves. Understand the basics, stick with it. Hunger for knowledge, because knowledge is power. You don't need to attend famous. universities, or burden yourself with piles of college tuition debt. You can learn anything you want to learn. It is a gift that you give yourself. Knowledge is portable. You take it with you everywhere. Just know that the smart will defeat the strong.

Be Creative In Nature

A skill which Tom Senkungu, a son of Aunt Florence who was studying his Bachelor's Degree in Medicine Makerere Univeristy from Mulago - Medical School joined us during holidays and wanted to explain to us more about creativity, truly everything was interesting...we couldn't resist since I lived with my sister in the teacher's quarters which was a walkable distance and it was safe for me to come any time I was required...had I lived in the different side of this school or nearby town I wouldn't participate in the debate.

He began by inspiring us that every-child is born creative, but our brains have been washed out by how we are brought up for example at school. The hard working and passion driven children always have thirsty for more success in their talents more than academics. By which some haven't been comforted; instead, they're greatly tormented and abused.

Students are torn between balancing books and talent. Can one concentrate on developing their talent and study at the same time? Or should one first study and discover their talent later? How about students who must use their talent in order to pay up their school fees and tuition? All these are questions a good number of students grapple with from time to time.

Some schools turn children into hard-drives for mere storage of information. If you have a choice between books and talent, weigh the situation, consult your family and learn when it is time to make a tactical withdraw.

I emphasize and advice you to balance both under close supervision of your role model. It is important to know that not everybody was born to be a President. It is important to first get to know and understand yourself so that you concentrate your youthful energies on what you can do best. Youthful energies are more like tools used in a garden to cultivate and harvest.

What makes it possible for people who might seem ordinary to achieve great things?

1. *Fact: More than 50% of all CEO's of most leading companies had 'C' or 'C' averages in college*

2. *Fact: Nearly 75% of all U.S. Presidents were in the bottom half of their school classes*

3. *Fact: More than 50% of all millionaires' or entrepreneurs never finished college....They All Had passion which Makes A Difference!*

There is more than one way to learn; never believe you cannot because the ability to learn is far, far more important than what you already know.

Remember that not having a clear goal may lead to death by a thousand of compromises; set your goal and start small but at the same time thinking big. Instead be thankful just like exams, every wrong answer makes you realise the right one.

Someone who intends to have a successful life, must be able to set goals and accomplish those goals. The common denominator for a truly successful life is to include wisdom, faith in a higher being, peace and understanding. Wisdom is the ability to have common sense and good judgment. Faith is an understanding that we are just part of the creation of something bigger than us that is unexplainable.

Success is never reached unless you have peace. Being able to have self-knowledge, and act according to what is in the best interest for our individuality and the people who surround us is wise. The reason why most of our leaders may not be old is because they are wiser and have more knowledge. They have lived longer lives, and they have more experience, which usually makes them have a better judgment. There is an old saying in the Spanish language: that the devil knows more for being old, than for being the devil. Success cannot be accomplished if one cannot take advice and learn from somebody else's mistakes. Wisdom is the ability to observe something and come to the conclusion of whether the results were good or bad.

Another common denominator for true success is the ability to be in touch with our own spirituality, to be able to look at ourselves, as small beings of a much bigger creation and know that our Creator is much bigger.
The latter makes us take decisions that not only benefit ourselves but also the people that surround us. Faith in a higher being is what makes us respect each other and fear to do wrong. Sharing, helping each other, and being able to love our descendant's future more than our own lives are all examples of how our spirituality makes us

successful.

I admit that a life spent making mistakes is not only more honourable, but more useful than a life spent doing nothing. That's why I excellently learnt the blessings of positive thinking plus the power of knowledge which promotes a sense of belonging that truly yields into gaining the strength for self reliance, that portrays Godly goodness of a man. The advantages of education, healthy living together with good behaviour in respect for life plus all benefits of hard work and frugality.

All these explanations became my basic principals in life till date. I completed my Primary Leaving Exams and went for my vacation while waiting for exam results. Early the next year, the exam results were announced. I was one of the best students in my school.

Without education, we are in horrible and deadly danger of taking educated people seriously. The person you will be in years to come depends on the information you feed your mind. Be picky about the books you read, the TV and Radio stations you tune in, the people you spend time with and the conversations you engage in?

Destroying any nation does not require the use of atomic bombs or the use of long-range missiles. It only requires lowering the quality of education and allowing cheating in the examination by students.

• *Patients die at the hands of such doctors*

• *Buildings collapse at the hands of such engineers.*

- *Money is lost at the hands of such economists and accountants.*

- *Humanity dies at the hands of such religious leaders.*

- *Justice is lost at the hands of such judges.*

The collapse of education is the collapse of the nation. This taught me generosity; your Candle Loses Nothing when it Lights another.

"No person was ever honoured for what he received. Honour had been the reward for what he gave." ~ Calvin coolidge, American President

"All that is not given is lost." ~ Robinranath Tagine, Indian Port

Don't allow the desires of what you have control you, put people first and regard money as a resource, develop the habit of giving. Be grateful for whatever you have. Everything is out there waiting for you, all you have to do is walk up and declare yourself in. No need for permission. You just need courage to say, "Include me"...When you discover your mission, you will feel its demand. It will fill you with enthusiasm and a burning desire to get to work on it; creative thinking is not a selfish act or a bid for attention on the part of the actor. It's a gift to the world and every being in it. Don't cheat us of your contribution. Give us what you've got. Time is free, but it's priceless. You can't own it, but you can use it. You can't keep it, but you can spend it. It can never come back!

PART TWO:
PERSONALITY

Personality

For someone to accomplish any higher achievement in life, through thinking there are basic qualities required to increase quantity. Personality is a set of qualities that make a person distinct from another. It's initiated in you from childhood. Through this trend, it's where favor wins luck, hard work yields profits, talents are discovered, patience pays, and it's where honest with integrity in behavioral characters are discovered. Self-management which includes self-control, trustworthiness, adaptability or being achievement orientated that result into good social skills like developing others, leadership, influence, discipline and responsibilities. The latter are values inculcated into us from childhood.

Your character opens doors the best education cannot. A good and positive attitude makes you see the bright side of life, become optimistic, and expect the best to happen. It is certainly a state of mind that is well worth developing in life and then finally cultivate a positive attitude regardless of your background, decide to adopt "strong" beliefs that create a good attitude rather than beliefs. Then your activeness, commitment, creativity, confidence, effectiveness, plans, progress, prayer, time, management, efficiency and lastly discipline or good habits will make you but bad habits will break you.

If I asked, "Are you living as a great thinker or or an ignorant person in modern lifestyle with self-destruction?" Indicators; gossip, marriage breakdown, revenge, corruption, child sacrifice and witchcraft:

1. Are you too needy or asking too much of your friends, constantly looking for their undivided attention without giving them adequate space?

2. Are you too volatile? Getting angry is a real turn off. Being intense or constantly seething about a situation is hard for others to deal with. The more you focus on how someone hurt you last year by making a mean statement, the more you will hold on to anger, negativity and resentment. All these take a whole lot of your energy for nothing in return. Perhaps the other person feels miserable, too. Perhaps they are holding a grudge against you. No one is happy that way. To forgive and forget is hard but pays well in the long run. You will be free from the shackles of the negative bond, and you have more room for better experiences in your life.

3. Are you too much blunt or intensive? Respect your friend's feelings, don't press or probe and make them feel uncomfortable. Thoughtful people are adaptable – they easily adjust themselves to accept what is not possible. If you're unhappy about something, notice how your ego holds onto it and won't let go of the fact that you cannot change it. This brings more pain that especially has to do with trying to control others or external situations. The person you can change through the easiest way is you. Happy people get that and bring their energy to what can be controlled – that is, they themselves.

4. Do you gossip, Do you ardently seek out private information about others. Then share it directly in order to make yourself feel better? You may feel well because of the trust of your friends. It may be tempting to gossip about others behind their back, but when you talk negatively, you take in the negative energy yourself. Think about the last time you spoke (or thought) badly of someone behind their back. How did you feel afterwards? Not overly enthusiastic, for sure. Instead, focus on others' strengths and positive habits and highlight what makes them special.

Wise people or great thinkers spend their time living a prayerful life, offer worship and serve God. They live as a role model socially and support the less fortunate. They exercise physically; have regular medical checkup and healthy diet. They finally expand knowledge and skills mentally, psychologically and have adequate rest. That's why I recommend you to read **Proverbs 3:13**...Happy is a man who finds wisdom, and the man who gains under-standing.

My alphabetical advice:

ABC

Avoid Boring Company

DEF

Don't Entertain Fools

GHI

Go for High Ideas

JKLM

Just keep a Friend like Me

NOP

Never Overlook the Poor and the suffering

QRS

Quit Reacting to Silly takes

TUV

Tune 'Urself' for your Victory

WXYZ

We 'Xpect' You to Zoom ahead in Life

Be Mindful

Mindfulness means being aware of something; paying attention for a purpose, that you must be present in the world, both outer and inner. It can help you train your brain to deal with your fears in more effective ways. Mindfulness can be learned by doing meditation. Meditation can make you aware of both your mental and exterior state.

A friend of mine once said in passing, "Oh, I am too busy living to think about life." These days you need to be always on, always plugged in, and always on the go. If you want to be stressed and unfulfilled, make sure you have no time to think, read deeply, reflect, have a proper perspective. Be mindful to everyone, you need to get good at making other people's problems your problems. It's not enough to listen to a challenge someone is facing; you need to take it upon yourself to solve it. It's not enough to support someone—you need to save them. Don't worry about boundaries. Make it personal. Own it fully.

Be Humble

In life, I relate everything I do to my purpose for a reason, but not compromise. I recall in March 2000 which was my entry year into Makerere College School, in my class (S.1 Red), some friends loved me enough to rebuke and tease me into silence for being skinny and having poor marks in some tests which psychologically tortured me. But deep inside me, I accepted no one's definition of my life and couldn't view my challenges as disadvantages. This reminded me about being more concerned with my character rather than my reputation; because my character is who I am while my reputation is what others think of me. I believed that every experience God had sent me must have a part in shaping how I act and think. I always wake up every morning with the thought that something wonderful was about to happen.

As you well know charity begins at home. I was raised to show respect. I was taught to knock before I open the door, say hello when I enter a room. Say please or thank you, and above all respect my elders. I'd let another person have my seat if they need it. Say 'Yes, sir' and 'No, sir' when they need me to, not to stand on the sidelines and watch, hold the door for the person behind me, say 'excuse me' when it's needed, to love people for who they are and not for what I can get from them but most importantly, I was raised to treat people how I would like to be treated by them; which meant being humble and respectful.

This principle greatly helped me to live an exemplary life, in every environment since I could not give in to bodily passions. I abstained from every sinful desire that attracted most teens. I'd follow my mentor's advice of being humble, no matter what the challenges or situation. God was and is my answer through prayer. I couldn't and I still don't miss church on Sundays.

One Sunday service, the preacher taught about equipping children and their upbringing from the Biblical scripture

2. *Timothy 3:14-17*; " 14 But as for you, continue in the truths that you were taught and firmly believe. You know who your teachers were, 15 and you remember that ever since you were a child, you have known the Holy Scriptures, which are able to give you wisdom that leads you to salvation through faith in Christ Jesus. 16 All scripture is inspired by God and is useful for teaching the truth, rebuking error, correcting faults, and giving instructions for right living, 17 so that the person who serves God may be fully qualified and equipped to do every kind of good deed."

Which he explained that God is the one who makes our families desirable and admirable through prayer, unless the Lord builds the family, we labor in vain *Psalms 127:1*

3. I learnt that when you pray, God is not mocked; for whatever one sows, that will he also reap *Galatians 6:7-9*. He related it to a parent and a child. If you asked your daughter/son studying in final year if that child is graduating, and child replies you, "Am not sure." Don't you feel disappointed for all the hopes you had in your son or daughter? Exactly that's how our Father in Heaven feels when we don't accomplish and follow his rules. Blessed are those who can laugh at themselves, for they shall never cease to be amused. I believe that great ideas from humble beginnings are like diamond crystals inside

a golden mine, hard to find...too useful, and impossible to hold onto.

Concentrate

I emphasized and dedicated my higher purpose in accordance to my will which meant carefully controlling all concentration into thinking for the best intention. Though it seemed challenging being introduced to 18 new subjects in high school, yet I was used to 4 only that is; Mathematics, Science, Social Studies and English. Yes, concentration was a key tool towards my progress but it required a lot of commitment and sacrifice.

My performance was average in class since there were smarter students than me in reasoning and I hadn't known how to balance my papers in every subject. Besides I would lead the class in only 5 subjects which were in my career interest, the rest were alternatives when choice is made but this didn't stop me from concentrating into other co-curricular activities like music since it benefited me with pocket money and allowances to supplement my fees.

Discover your Talent

Never let defeat suffocate your talent, I learnt not to be arrogant nor put my hope into issues which are uncertain, but decided to be responsible and understanding in discovering my talent. Most of us have various tremendous opportunities to do this as we are growing up but due to frustration and difficult circumstances, our talents are not utilized.

For example: Ask these two questions to school age children

1. What is your favorite subject at school?

2. At which subject are you best?

It's surprising that the young students will often give two different answers. They will say, "Oh, I get A's in Mathematics but I really like Science. Ooh, my favorite subject is History, but I'm better at Art. "

While I was in school, I privately began an in-depth study of what am good at and got incredible lessons on how to achieve my goal, since as a student I got good courage and strength; to look beyond the greatness of my task, guess why? I would borrow literature books from the school library like; Things Fall Apart, Journey to the Center of the earth, Adventures of Tom Sawyer, You are talented, Rich Dad and Poor Dad, The complete guide to writing non-fiction. On top of that I'd participate in music classes and as one of the students talented in music; I was given an invitation to perform abroad at Hilton hotel Arena in Zanzibar Island. Some students asked me,

"How did you make it?" Despite the difficulty or delay in achieving this success, I was shocked since it was a fully paid trip surprise!

I had to get more briefing from the music teacher, he told me that each of us had the obligation to present or have a valid passport and yellow fever immunization card two weeks before the departure date as we still train for the music-rehearsals. But I still doubted myself and further asked Mr. Busulwa (R.I.P), "Was this based on merit, attendance or participation?" Which he politely answered me that no. The school choir gave him an obligation to get participants who are honest, trustworthy with integrity to be trained and represent the school in the East African music festival and he recommended me amongst the first five because I rarely lied and don't gossip.

This impact proved me right that being humble and focused on your goal always gets results. Abraham Lincoln put it, "things may come to those who wait, but only the things left by those who hustle." I learnt that whatever I do, I do it with passion and not like how some lazy people who always complain of lack of luck. Did you know that most opportunities are missed by people because of pride?

I admire people who choose to shine even after all the storms they've been through. Whatever is good for your soul, do that. Be clear of what you really want.

I left Makerere College School due to my financial status. I had to look for another government school which was cheaper compared to the latter. My choice was Lubiri Secondary School situated along Wakaliga road since it had all subjects I had been studying. My clear goal was to continue with my education till I completed high school to join university. Remember, not having a clear goal may lead you to death by a thousand of compromises. Set your goal and start small as I did but at the same time think big.

I realised that successful people or great thinkers are ordinary people with extra ordinary amount of determination. The joy of succeeding in life, pressing towards the goal for the prize makes you forget what is behind and reach to what is ahead. Face your shortcomings. Remember nobody is perfect. Look for areas in your life where you need to improve and leave the character of, "To whom it may concern." Focus on the future and move on but don't live a dishonest life. Struggle to win and never count yourself as a loser, be determined to reach and purse your goal!

Someone who is a great thinker must be able to set goals and accomplish those goals. Those who don't make decisions never make mistakes, but remember actions speak louder than words. As you move through life set aside good ideas and share them with others for encouragement and inspiration.

Be Patient

Some people want to be entrusted with much long before they have been faithful with the little, this never works! My analysis of the life of King David from the Bible *(1 Samuel 16 to 2 Samuel 5)*... Anointed as the unknown shepherd boy, he demonstrated that he could fight off a bear and lion. On top of that, as a young man he killed the giant Goliath. Later, as a commander of Saul's troops, he learned warfare and leadership skills. It was only after many years and a variety of learning experiences that he was made king.

This taught me that if we are to improve our reputations, we must first recognise where we are on the journey and take things in their proper order. If I am a beginner then I must recognise it and learn accordingly. Even Shakespeare, Kiprotich, Mozart and Tiger Woods had to start somewhere. As Everson reminds us, "Every artist was once an amateur." Therefore, go step by step, don't seek to make an impact in one day.

Be Strong And Courageous

Accept no one's definition of your life; define yourself and never doubt yourself. A small group of thoughtful, concerned people can change this world...ask yourself, "Are you part of them?"

Don't fear; God did not give us the spirit of fear. I interpret "F.E.A.R" as... "False – Evidence – Appearing – Real."

Fear is a strong uncontrollable or unpleasant emotion caused by actual or perceived danger or threat. It hinders you from testifying or progressing.

Have the courage to say "No" or "Yes" when required but do not get depressed or isolate yourself. Feel honest with your life and be respectful because fear and joy are equivalent to confusion.

My experience might not be your experience; my challenges might not be your challenges. I conclude by saying, don't feel unworthy or isolated in whatever situation you're in and have self-confidence for it helps you do the right thing holistically.

Be strong you can come out bitter or you can come out better. There is purpose in your pain you never know who you're inspiring, for me I want to inspire people. I want someone to look at me and say, "Because of you...I didn't give up." The fact that you aren't where you want to be should be enough motivation, you can't have a Million-dollar dream with a minimum wage work ethic!

Be Honest

Honesty is a facet of moral character and connotes positive and virtuous attributes such as integrity, truthfulness, and straight forwardness of conduct, along with the absence of lying, cheating, theft, etc. Furthermore, honesty means being trustworthy, loyal, fair, and sincere.

It is important to be honest and tell the truth because people are more likely to give you a second chance if they have been able to trust you in the past. We all make mistakes, but lying will lead to more problems. Humility and honest personality breeds hard work which builds character.

'If you want to gather honey, don't kick over the bee hive'...I learnt this from Dale Carnegie

Professionalism

Professionalism is defined as the behavior you exhibit while at work and in public space (social media inclusive). As a professional, there are certain traits people expect to see in you regularly. Kindly find below few ways to be professional at work:

1) Punctuality: One of the personality traits of a good professional is arriving to work early.

2) Positive Attitude at Work: Every staff must come to work with a positive attitude. Be cheerful and look very bright with a smile. Don't carry your house problems to work place.

3) Dress appropriately at all times: Dressing is such an integral part of being a professional. Every staff must learn to dress properly at all times by putting on well clean ironed clothes, tidy hair, nice makeup, good perfume. Dressing professionally tells a lot about your person and will determine how people treat you.
You dress the way you want to be addressed.

Keep yourself professionally groomed and always pay attention to your personal hygiene.

4) Watch your Mouth: It is extremely important that we watch what we say, where we work, even to our students. As a professional, you must ensure the following: No Swearing, No Vulgar Language, No cursing, No fighting at Work, No shouting and behaving unprofessionally, complain less.

5) Share Knowledge: A true professional is always willing to lend a helping hand to his or her colleagues, shares knowledge and is always willing to assist fellow colleagues.

6) Respect for yourself and others: Every staff must respect himself or herself in the place of work. It is also important to respect your colleagues at work. Be polite at all times to fellow colleagues, even when provoked.

7) Control your anger: The work space is an area where you must learn to curtail your anger. Do not lie. Dishonesty never makes anyone look good. Be honest and calm at all times. Never expose your dirty linen in public. Professionals must ensure they do not expose their dirty linen in public. Avoid giving out too much information.

Keep confidential information confidential.

8) Follow Company Policies: Every true professional must obey all company policies. This goes to show that you are disciplined and respectful. Obeying work policies will be very advantageous to your career.

9) Get your job done: Ensure on a daily basis, you

prepared your **TO DO LIST** for the day and lesson plan for the week and strive to achieve them. At the end of every day and week, it's important to go through your to do list for the week and see how much you have achieved. Every professional must be **RESULT ORIENTED**

10) Look forward to each new day: A true professional looks forward to the opportunities that each new day brings. You shouldn't dread going to work, instead seek every opportunity to learn and grow on a daily basis.

Work Hard

Hard work always accomplishes something. You might learn something. You might be building something. It might be you to change something. But had work always gets results. It has been said "Some people dream of success while others wake up and work hard at it." Laziness doesn't result in anything but wasted time and resources. Do you want to see something happen? Work hard. I like the way Abraham Lincoln put it "Things may come to those who wait, but only the things left by those who hustle."

Hard Work Draws Attention

Want to get noticed? Work hard. The diligent stand out. We live in a culture that increasingly encourages and fosters minimal effort. Want to turn some heads today? Give 110% to whatever you are doing. It doesn't matter how many talents you have, or what you are called to do, do it with passion! Give it your heart! And soon the world will be watching. *"If a man is called a street sweeper, he should sweep streets even as Michelangelo painted, or Beethoven composed music, or Shakespeare wrote poetry. He should sweep streets so well that all the hosts of heaven and Earth will pause to say, here lived a great street sweeper who did his job well." ~Martin Luther King, Jr.*

Hard Work Brings New Opportunities

That is, hard work opens doors. The lazy complain about the lack of luck. Thomas Jefferson said *"I'm a greater believer in luck, and I find that the harder I work, the more I have of it."* Those who work hard find new opportunities always presenting themselves. Hard work is like an opportunity magnet. Sometimes these opportunities just seem to appear out of thin air, other times they come through new acquaintances, and often they are the result of greater insights and understanding that hard work produced in whatever the manner – hard work is usually the cause. Edison's famous words are relevant to this point: *"Opportunity is missed by most people because it is dressed in overalls and looks like work."*

Hard Work May Bless Others

No lasting benefit to mankind is achieved without hard work. The second greatest commandment is to love our neighbours as we love ourselves. We typically work hard to please ourselves. We should work harder to please others, bless others, and help others. Work hard, and don't worry about who gets the credit. Work hard and the world will be blessed. Such individuals are few and far between. Hard workers are worth their weight in diamonds. Horace Mann, the 19th century education reformer born in the state of Massachusetts, United States of America, once said, *"Be ashamed to die until you have won some victory for humanity."*

Finally trust in the lord. Avoid gossiping; don't tell people how big your challenges are, just tell your challenges how big your God is! You're a child of God, prosperity is your calling and not poverty. In **Jeremiah 29:11-12 (NKJ version)**, *"For I know the plans I have for you, they are plans for good and not for disaster, to give you a future and hope, in those days when you pray, I will listen."*

Trust In God

Another common denominator for true thinking is the ability to be in touch with our own spirituality. To be able to look at ourselves as small beings of a much bigger creation and know that our creator is greatly mighty than us, this makes us take decisions that not only benefit ourselves but also the people that surround us.

God commands those who are rich in this present world not to be arrogant nor to put their hope in wealth, which is uncertain, but to put their hope in Him, who richly provides us with everything for our enjoyment. He commands them to do well, be rich in good deeds, to be generous and willing to share. This way, they will lay up treasure for the coming age, so that they may take hold of the life that is truly life. *1Timothy 6:17-19*- Riches are the least worthy gift which God can give man. What are they to God's word, bodily gifts such as beauty and health, or to the gifts of the mind such as understanding, skill and wisdom?

God gives us many examples of how to think, then after pray to achieve our goal setting e.g. when Noah started hammering; his goal was to finish the ark. When Moses went to Pharaoh, his goal was to obtain release of the Israelites. When Joshua entered the Promised Land, his goal was to conquer it, bit by bit, battle by battle. When Solomon began construction, his goal was to build the temple. When Nehemiah explored the rubble around the destroyed Jerusalem, his goal was to rebuild the walls. This list could go on and on!

PART THREE:
BE FOCUSED

Focus

Being focused in your life enables you direct all your efforts towards achieving a particular goal. It considers the future with respect to your own plans or deeds, showing anticipation. But the closer you get to excellence in your life, the more friends you lose. People love you when you're average because it makes them average. When you pursue greatness, it makes them uncomfortable. Be prepared to lose some people on your journey.

Sometimes you have to move on without certain people; if they are meant to be in your life, they'll catch up. Remember other people are not loyal to you; they are loyal to their need of you. Once their needs change, so does their loyalty. Look at yourself and evaluate or assess on people you're with, whether they are true friends.

Many times, we are too quick to call everyone in our life genuine friends. Here's a profile checklist to help you identify genuine friends:

1. A true friend will enter into your experience. *1Samuel 23:16-18* Jonathan arose and went unto David in the wildness, Jonathan left his setting that was comfortable in the palace and went to a setting which is inhospitable to stand with his friend. He is willing to leave his contest of comfort to go stand with his friend.
A true friend can't stand in a long distance relationship in the sense that while you're
in the wildness I am praying for you but in need, "Prays with you." True friends show up and enter the wildness

with you. If by chance you've got a friend in your life that walks away whenever you're going through difficult hard times, am not recommending you that you cut them off but highly suggest that you check them out.

2. When a genuine friend shows up, they'll encourage you to endure. Some people can show up with the wrong disposition. Have you ever had that experience in your life?

A good example; remember Job's friends in the Bible, whenever they showed up, they used to complain and pour more grief, they try to find out what is wrong, so you've got to be careful. I don't need you to make a critical analysis over my life, when you show up just encourage me to endure. Do me a favor; if by chance in life, you have a friend who is that sort just keep him/her off.

3. A genuine friend is not envious of your elevation. **(1Samuel 23:16-18)** Jonathan said to David, *"I know you're in the wildness, but you are not going to stay here always, pull yourself together David. Fear not, maintain your spiritual swagger of God's protection. My father Saul knows very well that you shall be the next King of Israel and I am not tripping but all I want to do is to be next to you. I am not envious of your elevation; I know that God has already bypassed me by the principle of natural succession or kingdom protocol."*

If by chance you have a friend in your life who every time God blessed you to get a promotion, new car, or hand bag and they start tripping, I highly recommend you to cut them off and let them go. . They can't handle what God is doing in your life. Sometimes you need to have an usher's ministry, learn how to kindly escort such friends to the back roll seat of your life and you let them just watch you from a far because they can't handle being this close. If you're tripping of what God is doing to me right now, then what are they going to do when God multiplies all the blessings?

I found this so inspiring. Michael Jordan was born in 1963, in the slums of Brooklyn, New York. He had four siblings and his father's earnings were not sufficient to provide for the whole family. He grew up in a poor neighborhood. Exposed to mindless violence and heavy discrimination in the slums, he saw for himself only a hopeless future. His father saw in Michael, a lost soul and decided to do something. He gave Michael, who was 13 years old, a piece of used clothing and asked: "What do you think the value of this outfit would be?"

Jordan replied, "Maybe one dollar."

His father asked, "Can you sell it for two dollars? If you can sell it, it would mean that you are a big help to your family."

Jordan nodded his head, "I'll try, but no guarantee that I'll be successful." He carefully washed the cloth clean thou they didn't have an iron, to smoothen the cloth, but levelled it with a clothes brush on a flat board, then kept it in the sun to dry. The next day, he brought the clothes to a crowded underground station. After offering it for more than six hours. Jordan finally managed to sell it for $2. He took the two-dollar bill and ran home. After that, every day he looked for used clothing, washed and ironed it, then sold it in the crowd. More than ten days later, his father again gave him a piece of used clothing, "Can you think of a way you can sell this for 20 bucks?"

Aghast, Jordan said, "How is it possible? This outfit can only fetch two dollars at the most." His father replied, "Why don't you try it first? There might be a way." After thinking in his head for few hours, finally, Jordan got an idea. He asked for cousin's help to paint a picture of Donald Duck and Mickey Mouse on the garment. Then he tried to sell it in the school where the children of the rich study. Soon a housekeeper, who was there to pick his master, bought that outfit for his master. The master was a little boy of only 10 years. He loved it so much and he gave a five-dollar tip. 25 dollars was a huge amount for Jordan, the equivalent of a month's salary of his father. When he got home, his father gave him yet another piece of used clothing, "Are you able to resell it at a price of 200 dollars?"

Jordan's eyes lit up. This time, Jordan accepted the clothes without the slightest doubt. Two months later a popular movie actress from the movie "Charlie's Angels", Farah Fawcett came to New York for her Movie promos. After the press conference, Jordan made his way through the security forces to reach the side of Farah Fawcett and requested her autograph on the piece of clothing. When Fawcett saw this innocent child asking for her autograph, she gladly signed it. Jordan was shouting very excitedly, "This is a jersey signed by Miss Farah Fawcett, the selling price is 200 dollars!" He auctioned off the clothes, to a businessman for a price of 1,200 dollars! Upon returning home, his father broke into TEARS and said, "I am amazed that you did it My child! You're really great!" That night, Jordan slept alongside his father. His father said, "Son, in your experience selling these three pieces of clothing, what did you learn about success?" Jordan replied, "Where there's a will, there's a way."

His father nodded his head, then shook his head, "What you say is not entirely wrong! But that was not my intention. I just wanted to show you that a piece of used clothing which is worth only a dollar can also be increased in value, then how about us - living and thinking humans? We may be darker and poorer, but what if we **CAN** increase our **VALUE**?" This thought enlightened young Jordan. Even a piece of used clothing could be made dignified, then why not me? There is absolutely no reason to underestimate myself.

From then on, Michael Jordan felt that his future would be beautiful and full of hope. He went on to become the greatest basketball player of all times. How can I increase my own value? I am finding it a very interesting thought. I am sure, you too, will. What are you planning to raise your Value? Be Focused to think you can.

Persevere

In a competitive environment, perseverance is an invaluable asset. Be steadfast in doing something despite how difficult or how long it delays you in achieving success. Never let defeat suffocate you, there are times in life when your minimum effort will be noticed by no one and your maximum effort will be appreciated by no one.

Did you know that a river cuts through a rock not because of it's power but its Persistence? Do something today that your future self-will praise you for. Your ability to generate power is directly proportional to your ability to relax. Life is denied by lack of attention, reflect for a moment on what it actually might be like if your personal management situation were totally under control, at all levels and at all times. What if you could dedicate fully 100 percent of your attention to whatever was at hand, at your own choosing, with no distraction? It is possible. There is a way to get a grip on it all, persevere and get meaningful done.

Don't Worry About Things You've Already Lost

No matter how much you pay attention to the sunk cost fallacy, you still naturally gravitate towards it. The term Sunk cost refers to any cost (not just monetary, but also time and effort) that has been paid already and cannot be recovered. The reason we can't ignore the cost, even though it's already been paid, is that we are wired to feel loss far more strongly than gain.

Behind every successful person there's a lot of unsuccessful years, your best teacher is your last mistake.

Great. Now write down the very next physical action required to move the situation forward. If you had nothing else to do in your life but get closer on this, where would you go right now, and what visible action would you take? Would you pick up a phone and make a call? Go to your computer and write an e-mail? Sit down with a pen and paper and brainstorm about it? Talk face-to-face with your spouse, your secretary, your attorney, or your boss? *"Think like a man of action, act like a man of thought". ~Henry Bergson*

Was there any value for you in these two minutes of thinking?

If you're like the vast majority of people who complete that drill during my seminars, you'll be experiencing at least a tiny bit of enhanced control, relaxation, and focus. You'll also be feeling more motivated to actually do something about that situation you've merely been thinking about till now. Imagine that motivation magnified, as a way to live and work. If anything at all positive happened for you, think about this: What changed? What happened to create

that improved condition within your own experience? The situation itself is no further along, at least in the physical world. It's certainly not finished yet. What probably happened is that you acquired a clearer definition of the outcome desired and the next action required. But what created that? The answer is, thinking. Not a lot, just enough to solidify your commitment and the resources required to fulfill it.

Don't Believe In Memories More Than Facts.

Your memories are highly fallible and plastic. And yet you tend to subconsciously favor them over objective facts. The availability heuristic is a good example of this. It works like this: Suppose you read a page of text and then you're asked whether the page includes more words that end in "ing" or more words with "n" as the second-last letter. Obviously, it would be impossible for there to be more "ing" words than words with "n" as their penultimate letter (it took me a while to get that—read over the sentence again, carefully, if you're not sure why that is). However, words ending in "ing" are easier to re-call than words like hand, end, or and, which have "n" as their second-last letter, so we would naturally answer that there are more "ing" words.

Dream Into Reality

A dream is an imaginary event, hope or wish seen in the mind. Be careful who you share your dreams with. Successful people wake up when they are already focused and planned their day with big sustainable goals aligned to their strengths, while unsuccessful people are scrambling to figure out what they need to do next. The successful know what they are capable of and will invest all of their efforts in it, avoiding their weaknesses. Successful people aren't waiting around to be affected by economic trends. They are the ones who are creating the trends and making things happen.

Don't Dream Small

Somehow, we are conditioned to dream small. We are told to be careful of the challenge life throws our way. Successful people don't limit their dreams – they dare to dream **BIG**. They have a series of smaller, more immediate steps that will bring them to realise this goal. Having a bigger vision is important, but a step-by-step formula makes it more possible.

Thoughtful people love the concept of a mastermind where people share their challenges and come up with a list of solutions, or brainstorm ideas, using the group's synergy. They are life-long learners who push themselves out of their comfort zones. While most people think that when they graduate from college, they have finished learning, successful people remain students. They are constantly learning new things and have new experiences. They aren't afraid to try new activities and to fail at them. They are more excited about the journey than the payout. Successful people ignore get rich quick schemes. They are more focused on building sustainable careers through hard work, risk taking and creativity. They enjoy the journey despite the obstacles, because they are doing something that has meaning in their lives and makes a huge impact on their children's lives for generations to come.

Don't Listen To Dream-Killers

Be very careful who you share your dreams and plans with, especially if your ideas are unconventional or involve significant change. Whenever you change your own status quo - or even contemplate it – this brings up everyone else's stuff (a.k.a. fears). Many people will get a strange sort of satisfaction in telling you why something won't work, and will happily tell you about someone else who tried and failed spectacularly. Most worthwhile changes involve some sort of risk, and others will have failed trying. You could well be the one who succeeds. The only way to find out is to try. If you don't build your dreams, someone will hire you to help build theirs, wake up every morning with the thought that something wonderful is about to happen.

Don't Worry About Money

Almost everyone worries about money. Wealthy people are often afraid of risk or change because they're afraid they might lose what they have. The more financially challenged they are, they tell themselves they'll wait until they have "enough" or avoid risk because they're also afraid of losing the little they have. I'm not saying you should put yourself or your family at significant financial risk, but don't let money fears stop you from doing what you long to do. Odds are; you can find a creative way to make it happen on some level, or at least get started, no matter what your circumstances are.

Don't Listen to the Negative Voice Inside

You are not special, that voice you hear inside that dis-
courages you, belittles you, tells you you'll fail, tells you
to give up, tells you not to bother, is inside every single

Focus

person. Some of us have just learned not to listen, or
how to forge ahead anyway. When you step out of your
comfort zone (or even just think about it), that voice will
get louder. This is so predictable it's almost boring. Don't
let it stop you, it tries to stop everyone.

• Any time you sincerely want to make a change, the first
thing you must do is to raise your standards.
When people ask me what really changed my life eight
years ago, I tell them that absolutely the most important
thing was changing what I demanded of myself. I wrote
down all the things I would no longer accept in my life, all
the things I would no longer tolerate, and all the things
that I aspired to becoming.

Find A Mentor

One of the best ways to insulate yourself against failing
in life is to find and have a mentor, someone with experience who can guide and assist you.

Nothing is better than having a go-to person with whom
to discuss your ideas and contents.

You may be good at what you can do. But someone else in your field knows more than you do, has more skills than you do or has an extra edge. Nothing chases away

a slump faster than learning something new. Look for training sessions at universities or schools or workshops.

A Lesson To Learn For Business

During the press conference to announce NOKIA being acquired by Microsoft, Nokia, the Chief Executive Officer ended his speech saying, "We didn't do anything wrong, but somehow we lost." Upon saying that, all his management team including himself sadly concluded with tears.

Nokia has been a respectable company. They didn't do anything wrong in their business however, the world changed too fast. Their opponents were too powerful.

They missed out on learning, they missed out on changing, and thus they lost the opportunity at hand to make it big. Not only did they miss the opportunity to earn big money, they lost their chance of survival.

The message from this story is, if you don't change, you shall be removed from the competition. It's not wrong if you don't want to learn new things.

However, if your thoughts and mindset cannot catch up with time, you will be eliminated.

Conclusion

a) The advantage you had yesterday will be replaced by the trends of tomorrow. You don't have to do anything wrong, as long as your competitors catch the wave and do it **RIGHT**, you can lose out and fail.

b) To change and improve yourself is giving yourself a second chance. To be forced by others to change, is like being discarded.

Those who refuse to learn and improve will definitely one day become redundant, not relevant to the industry. They will learn the lesson in a hard and expensive way.

Have A Vision

Vision is the ability to see beyond the horizon of our comfort zone into the realms of our dreams. Visionary people plan well and have a long term view of where they see themselves not just in a few years' time as well as for generations to come. Create a vision, passionately own the vision and reliantly drive it to completion.

There is no way you will survive in this world without a vision; remember vision is prophetic.

Honestly if you don't know where you're going, the Lord will lead you there if you're focused *(Philippians 3:13-14)*. In the rhythm of life, at times we get off tune. However, remember that failing to plan is like planning to fail. The worst thing to being blind, is to have sight but with no vision.

Visions separate us. Look at people with whom you went to school with during your tender age till high school, where are some of them now? Your vision is what you will be tomorrow, a hint is "Don't marry a wife who does not know where you're going, just go your way." Some people don't know where you're going and they don't need to be your escorts.

A very good example in **Genesis 15:1-5**, "God's covenant with Abraham"…1, After this, Abraham had a vision and heard the lord say to him, "Do not be afraid, Abraham. I will shield you from danger and give you a great reward." 2, But Abraham answered, "Sovereign Lord, what good will your reward do me, since I have no children? My only heir is Eliezer of Damascus. 3, You have given me no children, and one of my slaves will inherit my property."
4, Then he heard the Lord speaking to him again, "This slave Eliezer will not inherit your property; your own son will be your heir." 5The Lord took him outside and said, "Look at the sky and try to count the stars; you will have descendants as that."

This teaches me that thou Abraham was 99 years old and his wife Sarah was 91years, his vision from God was to bear descendants that will inherit his property.

I grew up in a generation where everyone was going to USA – Europe or Emirates when seeking jobs, what you required was a ready passport. But the vision in my heart and passion wasn't in line with that, I was focused in developing my writing talent. I had the desire, will and aspiration to become the best author.

Some people see things as they are, and say, "Why?" Still others dream of things that never were and say, "Why not?" Thoughts are building blocks of life; Ignorance is not only a disease but it is also a disaster *(Proverbs 10:8).*

As the slogan goes, *"Great minds discuss ideas, average minds discuss events, and small minds discuss people."*

Very few people start off with many advantages, after realizing this quality that most philosophers, teachers, and experts agree about the importance of being focused. It's your focus that votes you off the lonely island of poverty, it is a key to the great life. This greatly impacted me on how to view things at some point.

I decided to discover exactly my intentions and interest; being specific and noting down my goals, I set a deadline for each goal using some reasonable time period. This made a list of everything I could possibly think of to achieve my goal. I had to take action for that plan immediately, to me that's the hierarchy of being focused with your vision.

The Zulu proverb says, *"copying everyone else all the time, the monkey one day cut off his throat."*

Be Innovative, Reflect And Act

Have you ever discovered that the difference between the poor and rich nations is not their age? Ok let's focus this in a larger perspective; this can be demonstrated by countries like India and Egypt, which are more than 2000 years old yet they're still poor countries. On the other hand, Canada, Australia and New Zealand which 150 years back were insignificant, today are developed and rich countries.

The difference between the poor and rich nation does not also depend on the available natural resources. Japan has limited territory, 80% mountainous, unsuitable for agriculture or farming, but is the second in world's economy. The country is like an immense floating factory, importing raw material from the whole world and exporting manufactured products. The second example is Switzerland; it does not grow cocoa but produces the best chocolates in the world. In her small territory she rears animals and cultivates the land only for four months in a year, nevertheless manufactures the best milk products. A small country which is an image of security, has made it become the strongest world bank.

Executives from rich countries who interact with their counterparts from poor countries show no significant intellectual differences. The racial or colour factors also do not evince importance: migrants who are heavy in laziness from their country of origin are forcefully productive in rich European countries. What then is the difference?

The difference is the attitude of the people, molded for many years by education and culture. When we analyse the conduct of the people from the rich and developed countries, it is observed that a majority abide by the following principles of life:

1. Ethics, as basic principles.

2. Integrity.

3. Responsibility.

4. The respect for Laws and Regulations.

5. The respect of citizen's rights.

6. The love for work.

7. The effort to save and invest.

8. The will to be productive.

9. Punctuality

In the poor countries a small minority follow these basic principles in their daily life. We are not poor because we lack natural resources or because nature was cruel towards us, we are poor because we lack attitude. We lack the will to follow and teach these principles of working to our new generation of rich and developed societies. Think about it...

PART FOUR:

DETERMINATION

Determination

It's the quality of mind which reaches definite conclusions. With it we start, but with an irrevocable agenda to go all the way. Life does not give you what you deserve; it only offers what you fight for and the future belongs to those who can breed passion, to encourage you into a personal commitment to great ideas for enterprises in the society. But if you fail to manage a kiosk, you can't manage a supermarket.

When launching a quest, you must be aware that victory is not given, it must be earned and that there are challenges to meet before achieving the prize. You must bear the affirmation in you that says, "If there must be a day when I shall lose or fail and be ashamed, it will not be today. Hey challenges, valleys and hills, I am coming for my victory and I am determined enough therefore, you shall deter-me-not."

Persistence and consistence

There is nothing on earth that cannot bow down or be affected or changed by a force that is exerted onto it, again and again and again. When you set a goal, and figure out what you have to do in order to achieve, then one of the toughest tasks begins, the task of persistence and consistence. The realm of failure is littered with names of people who dreamed big, who wrote down action plans and some took the first step but all in all failed to go all the way. Greatness is embedded in going all the way.

We become what we repeatedly do; success then is not an act but a habit. When you find out that a certain practice will help you achieve your goals, do it until it bears results. Destiny is attracted by the power of habit, because our habits later become the habitat of destiny when it arrives. If habit is a habitat for destiny, then it is a home, a house. One's destiny will always wander in space until he or she builds the required homestead for it. We must appreciate that success is a process. It takes time for one to be celebrated, to attain a great victory; it takes days, months and years because it's a journey. It may take 3-years to obtain a degree, a lifetime in politics, name it, but during that time there are things that must be unceasingly done in order to win, and they should be done persistently or consistently. Ask until you receive, seek until you find, knock until the door is opened. Let's dig deeper into this by exploring the do it section.

Do It Regularly!

The practices that develop us and cause our muscles to grow ought to be done regularly. Irregularity is an off-spring of not being serious and laziness, it culminates into failure. We always commune with destiny through the relevant practices; this fellowship must not be missed or postponed. What practice have you figured out, which if you did regularly would help you achieve your goals? Is it praying for an hour in a day, reading a book every month, devoting two hours of study every day, sleeping less, saving some amount of money every month, whatever it is, do it regularly it will benefit you in the long run?

Do It Purposefully!

Do not just do it anyhow, be reminded of the purpose and reason why you should do it every time you embark on it, then you will be strengthened to do it. You must have a reason for doing things, reasons that other people can't change. When you have no purpose, you will be forced to serve other people's purposes.

Do It No Matter What!

Situations will arise today, tomorrow or the other day, suggesting that you give it a break that you will not reap out of it, but as long you're sure of its benefits or results, make sure you do it. When it is time comes, let other things wait. Save the resting for tomorrow and do it. Do not give in to the voice that says, "I don't feel like doing it today."

Do It With Faith!

Do it with faith, being assured that the day of joy during harvest lies ahead and shall not tarry. Do it with confidence, allowing nothing and no one to intimidate or demoralise you, knowing that the time to work shall elapse and the time to earn shall commence in joy. Do it with undiminishing hope, rejecting whatever and whoever influences you to drop your tools, and give up, knowing that the job is yours to do but your will enjoy the destiny. It is those who labor who are entitled to hope. When you lose faith in the sowing, then you lose sight of the harvest. Faith is the substance of things unseen. Faith empowers our eyes to see, our hands to work and our feet to move.

Do It Improvingly!

You must refuse to be stagnant on the level at which you do anything. By doing it better every other day that you will continue to enjoy it and suck the benefits out of it. When you do the same every day, it becomes boring over time, and then you will start to hate it and lose interest in it. If you're a dancer, make sure you improve in your practices and rehearsals every day. Stretch yourself to learn something new whenever you do it. Exercise, revise, study, sing, speak, and write better than you did yesterday or the other week. The body can't live on one type of food every day. Likewise, you can't do the same thing the same way every day and expect better results.

Do It Passionately!

Don't waste your time doing it if you don't love it because you may end up wasting your life. It is passion which causes us to value and fight for the things we do and possess. Passion determines priority. It is how much you love it that you'll prioritize it. If I really love to graduate with first class honors, then I will prioritize it above everything, and if I must rest, watch a football match or do any other thing, it will be after I have read my books or done my research and assignments. He, who is not happy for the sowing seed time, will not smile in harvest time. Love it, delight in doing it, and be proud of doing it, then people will value it and respect it too. They will not labor to stop you or inconvenience you as you do it.

Be Men Of War Not Men Of Stature

Life is a campaign of conquest; the results we obtain from every battle become our total measure.

You must understand that becoming great is not something that we occur overnight, It is rather a process. One must rise through different levels in life. You must be tested and achieve victory. The victories you attain add up to earn you credit. It is due to how much credible you are that determines how high you rank above others, how needed and sought after you are in life. This is how you reign above others. Likewise, when your failures outweigh your victories, you end up being either less or not credited in what you do, you rank at the bottom; you are not sought after and are not needed. You therefore can't reign. Winning in every place, at every level, regardless of who you are or how old you are involves a battle. Great men have no distinct path to success. You must be ready to pass anywhere.

The quest to become great is not a battle, but a series of battles, fists and hardships all involved in one war. Those who overcome are decorated and can never be addressed with the same title with which they entered the war.

If the journey to greatness is a war, the winners then must be men of war. The question here is, "Who is a man of war?"

A man of war is a person who possesses an understanding of the dynamics of warfare, an ever-increasing volume or resource of fight and fortitude in spirit, capable of aiding him to go all the way in finding a desired victory, prize or crown.

From the above definition you'll realize that there are some major qualities that make a man of war and these are:

1. Understanding the knowledge of warfare.

2. Have an aspiration/desire/will.

3. No one will see value in you not until you see value in yourself.

4. If you want anything you've got to be a hunter.

5. Before you milk a cow, you've got to work for the cow first.

6. Bees will protect their honey, before you take it away from them.

7. Stop competing to be real.

8. Anything that comes up, let the man/woman in you roar.

9. Every good thing that comes to you must be through struggle. Read the Bible and learn the principles that make life a reality. *(Genesis 10:10)* Kingdom builders and vision bearers are fearless.

10. If you decide to be led don't seek to lead.

11. Spirit or heart of warfare, nothing physical, or plain ly to mention, nothing about stature. There are three elements that make a man of war and these include; spirit, speed and skill.

Did you know that there is no elevator to success, you have it take the stairs!

The heart, spirit of warfare/ the spirit of a warrior... The main ingredients that win a war, race or competition, the qualities by which great men gain access to victory and achievement are embedded in their inner man; the spirit. I say this because victory is first spiritual before it is physically manifested, it is first invisible before it is made visible. Therefore, one must possess in him the necessary abilities to transform the victory from its state of intangibility to tangibility.

What qualities or ingredients are these?

Acquire The Heart Of A Lion

We can't avoid likening (comparing) our areas and spheres of struggle to ambition in the wild life setting. The absolute law of the jungle is you are either the predator or the prey. The predator will always have the leadership, satisfaction, and respect from the prey. It's a system that awards survival for the fittest necessarily not through size or strength, but proportionally to those, which are intelligent prove to be greater.

The difference between animal jungle and human jungle is that animals were created in their distinction by God. The lion was made a lion and the antelope an antelope. What amazes me about the human jungle is that God created all of us just as humans; we choose either to be a lion, snake, rabbit, and bull whatsoever. We choose to be predators or prey.

The achievers of this age must develop in themselves the heart of a lion, the king of the jungle. The lion is one of those animals which are disadvantaged in size and height but what makes it reign over the rest, is its heart and spirit. You can only best describe a man of war by aiding yourself with the character of a lion in the wild. Let's look at the qualities that make a lion or man of war special among many.

Fearlessness Or Bravery

1. In the jungle, which animal is the biggest? I under stand it's an elephant.

2. In the jungle, which animal is the tallest?
I understand it's the giraffe.

3. In the jungle, which animal is the wisest? I under stand it's the fox.

4. In the jungle, which animal is the fastest? I understand it's the cheetah.

Amongst all these wonderful qualities mentioned, where is the lion in the picture. Yet you say the lion is the king of the jungle even without any of these qualities. But I discovered something fascinating about the lion.

The lion is courageous, the lion is very bold, and the lion is always ready to face any mountain, any challenges, and any barriers that cross his part, no matter how big they are. The lion walks with confidence. The lion dares anything and it's never afraid. The lion believes he is unstoppable. The lion is a risk taker. The lion believes any opportunity is worthy giving a trial and never allows it slip from his hands. The lion has charisma.

What is it that we get to learn from here?

1. You don't need to be the fastest

2. You don't need to be the wisest

3. You don't need to be the smartest

4. You don't need to be the most brilliant

5. You don't need to be generally accepted to become your dreams and be great in life

All you need;

a) is courage

b) is boldness

c) is will to try

d) is the faith to believe it is possible

e) is to believe in yourself that you can do it

The lion has unmatched character, infinite abundance of fearlessness and bravery in the jungle. It has no iota (inconsiderable quantity) of fear for going for what it wants. It is not intimidated by size, looks, height and noise etc.

Winning is a portion to the fearless; fortune favors the brave. There will always come a time in life when there is no door but a wall, and the brave remain to break through to the better end. The first content of character that any battle tests is bravery.

Why am I talking about battles, bravery? Why am I militarizing this? There are hundreds of people in the world who want to be better than you, who want to rule over you, this makes it a competition, a race, a battle. Competitions call for competitors, races require runners, wars crave the indulgence of warriors. For every ambition there's opposition, for every good will, a bad will.

Fear must be erased out of your vocabulary and mind. There's one major reason why men fear, they fear to lose. We fear to lose. This is because when you venture into a race and lose, the loss will destroy many things you originally had. For example, if you don't win, you may lose life, friends, respect, glory, time and etc.

If you fear to lose you will lose to fear, never enter into any battle already as a loser. The moment you accord fear an abode in your spirit, you add to yourself an enemy living alone the one that's waiting for you in the battle field. You begin the competition in a damaged state, and fight against a foe that's so fresh. You must never fear and expect to win. Fear exploits our ores of strength and ability to win.

We should rather embrace losses and failures as an opportunity to learn, re-group, re-organize, re-strategize, because we now know how strong the battle is, and the mistakes that orchestrate defeat.

Bravery is the principal resource. Intelligence is the fundamental resource. History is littered with men who conquered territories at a disadvantage of numbers and armory yet with an abundance of bravery. It is our will to fight to death that enables us to win, other factors and provisions only aid us.

Are you brave enough to start? Are you brave enough to go all the way? Darkness lives behind light, failure behind success and death behind life, there are times you'll need to face death in order to find life. Every progress calls for a better show of bravery. You may need to brave the cold to work all night to transform your financial status; you may need to be brave enough to suffer low expenditure for a time in order to save enough to make a big investment. Some folks are trampled upon and minimized in certain areas just because they are not bold enough to use their rights or even speak out their mind and ideas.

Most of the people who rule us or decide the course of things are not the wisest, or highly privileged, but because of their bravery they manage to gather support from other people. Do you think M.L King was the most qualified man to lead the fight to black equality? Probably no, but he had enough courage, the bravery to speak, to persist, to demand, even when he knew it would take his life and this is what other people who would have managed to do it feared most... To be beaten, imprisoned or even killed, but M.L King fought and won a battle against men who had guns, authority and numbers. This must teach you that there's a weapon stronger than machines, a brave minority is to be feared more than an armed majority. The world has not experienced anything impossible to the brave.

No man is born brave, it is just built. Even a lion must learn to hunt. You start with being bold among your friends, at school, home, place of work, in your small circles.

Bravery is tested and built-in times of adversity. Gold is tried in fire and acceptable men in the furnace of adversity.

Your bravery must overshadow your weaknesses; you must never feel intimidated by those who appear more worthy to win, because of their money, connections, fame. The prize does not compete for men; it is always the other way round. Bravery is like electricity without it, TVs, fridges, lights, cookers can't work. Without bravery you can't endure, persevere, and apply knowledge. In simple terms, you may not be able to use other abilities and resources available just because of fear.

PART FIVE:

CHOICES MATTER

Choice

Greatness is birthed by choice. The rift between the admired and their admirers is formed by the opposite choices made in their day to day lives. Choice does not process greatness; it rather ignites you and sustains you on the journey to greatness. Choice is a seed, if not planted, a fruit shouldn't be expected. Of what profit would it be to a man, who sits in a full tank fuelled car, highly serviced, excellent in condition, yet he refuses to fix the key and turn on the engine. Such a man must never expect to move.

Choice is a fire, when we choose; we start a fire in us which burns away the mentality that would not act and fulfill the desires of the choice made. This fire creates an overwhelming thirst in our soul which can only be quenched by results, victory and achievement. Man will then seek to gather necessary resources within and outside his body in order to quench this thirst.

Choice determines thirst, thirst determines work to be done, work done determines size of achievement or victory and in the end, the achievement sets you apart to reign over the failures and the mediocre life. Choices have the ability to add, subtract, and divide or multiply. Life sums up into the choices we make day in day out.

The Choice to reign...I believe reigning is not a portion to those who make simple and lowly choices but those who choose to navigate the hard but credible sea routes to greatness. Therefore, if a man must reign, he has to make the choice, "the choice to reign."

Choices are different from thoughts. Out of many thoughts we always select one which we are willing to execute, this becomes a choice while the rest become talk. In simple terms, a choice is the sum of a thought and a will. Thoughts alone do not create a thirst to achieve but when aided by a will, the fire to achieve is started.

I and my Old boy Brian while still at Makerere College School admired to become doctors; I had the thought but not the will. Brian on the hand had the thought and the will to become a doctor. He reigned over me because he made the choice. He always had a thirst to achieve. It was vivid in his hard work, and he was always reading; never missed on doing his assignments and he eventually graduated with an 'A' in sciences which enabled him get a government scholarship to study till 2014 when he got his doctorate in Tropical Medicine from East London University compared to me who opted for Engineering from Aptech and then Middlesex University. Many people talk about reigning but are not reigning in actual sense because all they do is to think about it but never make the necessary choices about it.

Many of us know that Neil Armstrong was the first man to step on the moon, but we don't know who the second, third, or fourth was. This is not because we don't research, the world only cares about who is at the top, people want to assimilate and associate with the cream.

This century belongs to people who choose to lead. Choose to lead whether in a small group, community, district, region, nation, even in the whole world. If you choose to lead, you will always extract and invest the maximum of your potential in what you do. We only invest as much as we choose not what we possess, yet investment determines harvest. I can tell the magnitude of your choice by assessing your efforts. Ever wondered why brilliant students read the most even when they already know a lot, why rich men sleep less and work harder even when they possess great wealth? Or have you ever wondered why weak students read less or don't mind yet they know nothing, why poor men sleep a lot, work less yet they literally possess nothing. The answer traces back to the choices they make.

One makes a choice to seek knowledge while the other chooses to be ignorant; one makes the choice to work and gain mass wealth while the other chooses to stay poor. It is the difference in thirst to achieve and the post-activities done that create a divide, rift between them. Then we have the rich and the poor, the leaders and subjects, knowledgeable and ignorant.

We are responsible for our success or failure. Your first duty in the quest for greatness is to make the relevant choices. You can't blame anyone for any result upon whose conception you had the right to choose. Every man is culpable for the consequences conceived by the choices he makes, whether positive or negative.
Choice making is not a respect of background, strength, wealth, status and the like. The receptionist in the world of choice has one command to follow that is to welcome everyone. Everyone is qualified to choose.

Assign yourself to make a research on a sample of about ten successful people you know of in any field, be it politics, business, music whatsoever. You will understand this. That their backgrounds may not have been the same, some looked more deserving or worthier but choice put them in the same status quo. Since many of us are familiar with American history, let's take a short case study there.

George. W. Bush (Jr) was a son of a former President and knew what the white house was like, he was well known by many politicians or American citizens. In many cases, he seemed to have had the right background and beginning. Every one wasn't surprised for his desire to be President. He chose to be and finally became. Barrack Obama on the other hand grew up on the other side of life; his background was littered with facts that presented him unworthy of the presidency to the lay man. Born of a poor Kenyan, raised up by a struggling American mother, a pure African American involved in smoking marijuana at a youthful age, a simple little-known senator from Illinois. What qualified Barrack Obama? What made him reign? What made George W. Bush reign instead of the other sons of the rich and popular? Choice, 'the choice to reign', When two people are pursuing the same prize, the one with a greater thirst will achieve it.

Choice is a distinguisher; it sieves the extra ordinary from the ordinary. You will never rank highest if you don't make the highest choices. You can never stand out if you don't make outstanding choices. The world is a stair case.

The best time to choose to reign is now. I implore you to think and choose today. Your abstinence from choosing to reign can cost you a destiny and make you a servant. Choose today, to improve, to be better, to go for a Master's Degree or a Doctorate, to submit to a senior, to save much more than you spend, to invest more, to make your company, clinic or school the best in the country, sow this seed of choice. Many people die poor yet they would have been rich, many people die rich yet they would have been richer.

The choice to reign gives you the thirst to climb to the top, and the thirst to stay at the top. It is the hungry python that hunts.

When you make master choices you attract submissiveness from people who choose mediocrity. People will always follow he who is thirstier for victory than they are. When you have a big dream, people will follow and support you because they are sure your dream will give birth to their small dreams.

Choice to live

I know this may sound ridiculous. You should be asking how now; How do I choose to live? The hope of success in thinking belongs to the living, since this helps someone to learn from his/her past mistakes. I choose to live by choice, not by chance. I choose to excel, but not compete. I make changes, not excuses.

What life experiences have led you to devalue yourself? Get angry enough to do what it takes to reverse the losses you suffer as a result of devaluing yourself? Older people can offer valid thoughts about life; experience does have value. Don't devalue yourself because you do not enjoy joining a large, enthusiastic, happy business class.

"What price do you pay for feeling the way you do? No price is too high to pay for the privilege of owning yourself"— Friedrich Nietzsche. How many times each day do you mean to say one thing, and say another, do you dress the way you want to dress? Be who you are and say what you feel, because those who mind don't matter and those who matter do not mind. My great passion is showing people how surprisingly easy it can be to create a fulfilling life they deeply love. You don't necessarily have to make radical, risky changes to have a much richer, joyful experience of life, but you do have to take the steps that move you forward into new ways of doing things.

Whether your life needs some minor tweaks or you long to take huge leaps, here are some of the most common habits, beliefs and attitudes that can block you from experiencing the positive change you long for: as Nelson Mandela said; there is no passion to be found playing small - in setting for a life that is less than the one you are capable of living.

Choose Telescopically

Man's mind is endowed with two distinct invisible visual apparatuses. These are; the telescope and the microscope. The mind, at the bearer's order can either serve you telescopically or microscopically. The mind has the ability to focus on distant situations (the future), bring them nearer and magnify them such that we assess them in the present age. You can simply say the mind is a gateway to the future, through it we visit tomorrow, collect necessary information, and prepare ourselves for the future by making relevant choices today.

If you desire to reign in this century, you must learn to employ both apparatuses while making choices.

Let's discuss why we should and how to apply the telescopic abilities of the mind in making choices. This is what I call choosing telescopically:

1. If you hope to reign in this century, you must develop in yourself the ability and habit of making choices with prior knowledge to what the impact of their resulting consequences will be in the future. In simple terms reigning does not belong to the opic (short sighted). Making a choice is like adding a brick onto the building

of life. It is easier to add a brick than to remove it from a building. And when you patch the hole up,
it will not hide but always appear that something had gone wrong there. When making choices, we have the time and right to fly into the future, to find out by way of reasoning, research and consultation, whether the future will grant us reward or my remorse incase the choices we
make today are pursued to realization.

2. It is suicidal, if not silly; to run after a choice without first visualizing on what will happen to you, your assets, or the people around you, in hours, days, months or years after it has been brought to fruition.

3. Have a telescopic mind, think, and see what gain or profit your choice will bring. The stuff of today will pass away with it having sown a seed
into tomorrow. I've seen people make stupid choices and end up reaping thorns and thistles in the future. The same have one common
statement to say, "I wish I had known."

4. I've also seen and heard of people who made choices, being sober and knowledgeable of what's in stock for them in the future. Those are the great men we know. Because they chose telescopically, they predicted and were forearmed for the challenges that lay ahead, and prepared themselves for receiving victory.

5. Great men have a special ability of foresight. They first envision what the future holds before they make a specific choice. They'll start a business with the goal to have it live for a century or through generations. They see the

world and themselves in many days from now.

6. Before you venture into a business, first ponder where it will have taken you in the next ten, twenty, or more years. A great mind will start a shop with a goal to raise it into a supermarket in 5 years, while a poor mind will start the same shop without any idea or vision of what he wants it to be in 5 years. See the difference?
The poor mind is looking for daily bread in the business, he / she wants to keep himself from starving and the boredom of unemployment while the great mind envisions increases which take his financial status to another level, he is choosing telescopically. If you are to trail these two people's financial ways, you'll find out that the great mind saves more from his profits and reinvests more compared to the poor mind, the wise man's books of records will be more organised compared to those of the poor mind, if he even cares to keep records. The great mind is looking for satisfaction, while the poor mind is looking for survival. After five years these two will be different in financial status, one will desire to serve the other.

7. Before embarking on a journey, be it politics, business, a degree, whatsoever, ask yourself some questions; "What will I become in this? What will I gain? Will I become any better? What are the advantages and disadvantages of the choice am making?"

8. We always fail and quit because we did not fore see. With fore sight, you will not be swayed and discouraged by storms and the challenges found on the way. We've seen and heard of people who enter into politics and quit the game after one or two failures. They didn't look

through the telescope and see losing an election as one of the hits and tides that are involved in the journey.

We've also heard of those who envisioned it all from the start, armed themselves with courage and persistence, set their eyes on the prize, stood up from every fall and finally achieved great heights a good example; Nelson Madiba Mandela's long walk to freedom in South Africa. It would be wrong to say that America's 16th President was not telescopic in choosing to be an American politician.

He walked through every failure and fire as if he had foreknown of its coming. Failing twice in business, overcoming a nervous breakdown, and loosing eight elections and finally winning a presidential election teaches us one thing, that he put the map on the table, saw the mountains and valleys, the stormy oceans to be sailed, the straight and crooked roads to be walked, presidency, estimated the price to be paid with all prior knowledge and bravery, he chose thus to embark on the journey to the white house.

NB: (God & Man), Before God created man; He first focused into the future, seeing this man existing, thought about what he will need to survive, will he live in space or on earth? Will he need to eat or drink? Will he need shelter? What other creatures will he have to co-exist with? By asking Himself such questions and many more He was be able to choose telescopically. That's why he analyzed and found out that there was need to create an Eden before man.

A non-telescopic thinker or planner will choose to create man and right away start. These two consequences will likely befall him, he will either not be able to finish the creation because he's thinking that it didn't enable him to gather enough raw materials, and if he succeeds in creating man, the man will live just a few days and die because the creator didn't provide food for his creation. This is the main reason why we usually fail to start great things and even when we start them, their life span is so short that they die without fetching us the desired glory.

Choose Microscopically

Like I discussed earlier, the mind can serve us telescopically or microscopically. Let's discuss why we ought to and how we should apply the microscopic abilities of the mind before making choices.

In our day to day lives, we apply a microscope to view objects, small or big, because it magnifies anything by several hundred times. In a like manner, the human mind has the potential to view and analyze in depth the details of an object or situation at hand and bring it to magnification, realization and comprehension even the minutest element in the vicinity of focus. If you can't see what exists today, you can't see what the future holds. The need to analyze the future arises from the details we have about the present. Success belongs to those who have the ability and habit of studying the present, the current trend or tide of affairs.

Allow me to explain this concept using an example of a monkey, sweet banana and money. If you put bananas and money in front of the monkeys, Monkeys will choose bananas...since they don't know that money can buy a lot of bananas.

IN REALITY; if you offer a **JOB** and **BUSINESS** to some people, they would choose a job because most people do not know that **BUSINESS** can bring more **MONEY** than Wages. Similarly, *Robert Kiyosaki*, author of the bestselling book *"RICH DAD, POOR DAD"* and also a business partner of Donald Trump said:

~ *One of the reasons the poor are poor, is because they are not trained to recognise Entrepreneurship opportunities. They spend too much time in school and what they have learnt in school is to work for wages instead of money working for them. Profit is better than Wages, for wages can make you a living but profits can bring you a fortune. Think about being an entrepreneur and stop fighting over increments of salaries, it still won't be enough.*

The Dont's Of Choice

Don't choose under pressure

Pressure exists for just a time. But the decisions made under pressure are regretted during times of calm. Pressure is a force; its sole intention is to disturb your speed or stability. You realise that when you are under pressure, things will appear to move or do fast, you'll think you have no time to think or consult before making a choice regarding an issue. Pressure will always create a tense atmosphere around you, it will want to pull or push you into making rush decisions without giving keen regard to the facts and future. During such times you ought to settle down alone, create a peaceful environment in which you can make a good decision. Remember, "You rush you crush." Pressure will give you its own options or even tell you that, "There's only one way out of this." And usually its options are the disastrous, poisonous sugar-coated cakes. You must know that pressure has no rule over us unless we allow it. Pressure is an agent of evil. Pressure and calm co-exist like light and darkness; you never know that one is present unless the other departs. When university exams are approaching and they say you won't sit for them unless you've paid, if you happen to submit to pressure, you can end up doing regrettable things

just to acquire the money, like stealing, prostitution and when you realise the trouble you have caused yourself by solving a problem, usually the later tragedy will be greater than the initial one. For example; you can be imprisoned and miss the exams, or even contract

HIV/AIDS by having sex with a rich but infected person. Teach yourself to disregard pressure and make choices as if it were absent.

Don't Choose Under Guilt

That you made a mistake in the past does not mean that you should stay bound by guilt forever. All of us make mistakes, but winners overcome the guilt and move on with life, failures continue to linger in their past, revisit their mistakes not to learn from them but to entertain the voice that says, "You are unworthy to move on." I've seen girls drop out of school due to pregnancy, and they later refuse to go back to study after giving birth because their guilt makes them feel ashamed and no longer fitting in school. They choose a life of low education resulting to poverty. I don't care how much of a thief you were in your community; as long as you're sure that you have reformed. I believe you have the moral feet to stand for a leadership position there. It is incumbent upon you to choose whether to meet the future either as who you are or who you were. Some people will use guilt to take you hostage and persuade or even force you to follow their will against your will. It's not wise to make choices because you feel indebted to someone. Many of us have traded our feelings, destinies, happiness and the truth under such circumstances.

Don't Choose Under Excitement

There once lived a king who usually had feasts in his palace. His wife's daughter was a great dancer. The king so invited her to entertain him, his guests and officials at one feast. This young girl did what she was good at, then at the end the king was so happy and excited about the dance; stood up in front of everyone then said to the young girl, "Ask for anything and I shall grant it", that wasn't bad, but the last segment of the statement was even if it's half of my kingdom. For a king who is aware that every promise he makes must be fulfilled this was the stupidest thing to say. Fortunately, or unfortunately the girl asked for John the Baptist's head. But what if she had asked for half of the kingdom? This king would have reduced his son's inheritance by half, jeopardized all his forefathers' efforts to make the kingdom what it was before he became king, created an enemy nation just next door, the list would be endless. All this would have occurred because of a silly king who made a reckless choice due to excitement. Excitement does not last forever, it's short-lived. You become sober after a few hours and realise you've made choices that you can't bear. You go to a party, get soaked in the joy, get hooked up with a girl, impregnate her and later realise you have to become a father before you finish high school. You throw your savings into a business without doing serious research just because a friend has told you how it has made money for him in a few days only to end up losing because you acted on excitement and forgot to apply business acumen.

Don't Choose Under Anger

Fury is a fire. Remember fire is one of those things which cause irreversible change. It is an agent of fatal destruction. Those who make choices under the influence of anger usually apply fire where water is required. Instead of cleaning, they burn and when the veil of anger falls off their brains, they realise that they now have only ashes of what were good relationships, friends, careers, to mention but a few. You don't need months to destroy or lose what took you years to build or acquire. It takes less than an hour's argument to break a ten-year-old marriage.

Now I think there are two kinds of anger, righteous anger and evil anger. The former lights a desire in you to create positive change about something while the latter which am talking about in this segment promotes evil and moves you to act wickedly.

Those who hope to reign in this era must learn to subdue their fury or anger and deny it access to their chambers of decision making. What you sow is what you reap, if you sow fire while choosing, you reap fire in the consequences. Evil repels good. If a man has no good in him, he cannot acquire gold because men will travel from the ends of the earth and lay their gold at the feet of a man who has good in him. By good I mean, good speech, counsel, ideas, knowledge, and character, to mention but a few.

You won't be excused in court by pleading that you shot your spouse dead because you were angry...

Don't Choose Under Ignorance

In law, ignorance of a crime doesn't call for the criminal to be pardoned. Life also operates in that manner. If you hope to reign, you should desist from making uninformed decisions or choices. Do not venture into something you know little or nothing about. Don't let other people do the knowing for you, knowledge only benefits the bearer. Like the living say good morning, "I wish I knew" is a common greeting among failures and losers. It hurts and usually doesn't change anything for one to acquire knowledge when its need and time of necessity is passed. Knowledge, time and success must co-exist and grow together. Failure arises when they part ways.

Don't Choose To Please Men

The ultimate law of choice is, "Consequences befall the maker of the choice". Since the consequences will be yours alone to handle, you mustn't seek to please any one. Just in case you fail, it is the same people you sought to please who will be the first to fix the blame on you. It is by living life the way that pleases you that will make you proud. You can't live a thousand lives. It is okay to consult others but giving you advice is all they should do. When it comes to making the final choice, you need to sit alone and consider the advice you have been given including other relevant factors and make a fitting decision. The people we want to please sometimes become our points of weakness especially in times when we have to make hard choices.

Many people fail to walk rewarding journeys because they imagine a friend or relative will not be happy about it. If you are sure in your heart that you are making the right decision, it then shouldn't matter what the rest will think or say. You should learn to be independent minded, and everyone around you must be aware that you are not the type that dances to other people's tunes. No or yes should sprout out of your mouth with an "I mean it" sense.

By pleasing people, you end up walking in their shadow, wasting time in fulfilling their selfish ambitions. It means collecting crumbs from someone's table yet you have the ability to set your own table. "We are all indebted to please but one person, GOD. He will never assign us to please anyone else, for He never shares his glory."

CONCLUSIVE REMARKS

Have you realised some choices which were made without the future in mind? Sometimes those choices bite us in our mid-life which may result into regrets when we're older, like:

1. Marrying The Wrong Person:

When you're young, check your motives for marrying. Don't marry to copy your peers, or for social standing or out of pressure. Marry for love and companionship, marry the right person, marry your best friend. For if you marry the wrong person or for the wrong reasons, you will have to put up with that person the rest of your life. Things might get worse between you two; then depression, physical abuse, affairs, pain, shame, court cases, bitterness will define your mid-life years all because you chose the wrong one. Things will get worse when children are involved. Make the right choice of a spouse when you are young.

2. The Opportunities You Did Not Seize:

When you are younger many doors will open, you will get many chances. Many young people let these opportunities go because of fear, laziness, or pride; yet well younger and with more energy is the best time to start a venture and a name for yourself. Some think the opportunities are too big for them. Take advantage of them or one day when you're older you will want to go back and grab those missed chances.

3. The Bridges You Burned:

When we are younger, we care little for relationships, what most think about is getting money and moving up the ladder of success at all cost. Many use and trample on people to progress, they take relationships for granted, messing up bonds, sleeping with people for personal gain. But these bad actions will catch up with you ahead. When you will realize how empty life is without love and friends or when you will have success but no one around you or no one to trust you.

4. The Child You Aborted:

You are a young lady; you get pregnant and you are scared. You take the aborting option quickly thinking of that moment then. But when you are much older, you will look back and wish you kept that baby. When you will be rich and successful you will wish that child you gave up on would be around to enjoy the fruits of your hard work. Being a single mother doesn't mean you can't make it in life or you can't find a man in future.

5. The Child You Rejected:

Young man, you impregnated a woman, she told you she's pregnant with your child. You rejected her and the baby and ran. But years later when you're 50 something, you will wish you were responsible, you will wish you manned up and became a father to that child. You will see that child excel and become an adult but will have no claim to that grown child who you rejected from the beginning. You will regret being a Dead-Beat Dad by choice.

6. The Marriage You Destroyed:

So, you get married to your good fiancé; the first months in marriage were good but shortly after, with your money and charm, you started having affairs. You became unfaithful. Your spouse begged you to stop, your children started hurting, your marriage was collapsing. One day when you are older, it will hit you how foolish you were to destroy the good marriage you had begun to build for mere temporary thrills in affairs that did you no good. You will realize the damage you caused to your children and spouse.

7. The God You Disowned:

When you are much older you become wiser, God becomes more real as you see life in a more meaningful way. But don't wait to get older to start enjoying a relationship with God. Know God when you are young, build your future with God. Don't be a young rebel who runs back to God when age catches up with him/her.

8. The Body You Messed Up:

You have only one body to live with all your life. The cigarettes, the alcohol you are abusing, the drugs you are taking, the unhealthy food you're consuming; all that will destroy you slowly. When you are 50 and lifestyle diseases catch up with you, you will wish you took care of your body when younger, that you exercised more; but now the damage is done.

9. The Time You Wasted:

The time you are wasting when younger in worry, wrong relationships, laziness, being a couch potato, giving excuses and pursuing meaningless things; you will never get it back.

10. The Dreams And Talents You Shelved:

Are you talented when young? Are there things you love to do and you are good at them? Nurture those talents, exploit them, don't give up even if you encounter setbacks, don't give up on your dreams. If you give up, when you're older you will look at your peers who stuck to what they love and made it and think to self, "That could have been me". Pursue a career, study a course you love. Don't waste years of your life in a field that doesn't fulfil you.

11. The Name You Defamed:

When you are older, a legacy is very important, the value of your name is crucial. You will ask yourself what is your reputation, what are you leaving behind? Your legacy is a sum total of your actions since youthful days. We write our biography by how we live life every day. When you look back your path and you see the mud you threw at your own name, the shame you attracted and the little value you have added to the world; you will regret.

12. The Wealth You Threw Away:

Are you riding on good money during your productive years? Earning good money? Don't throw away that mon ey in clubs, reckless living and wasteful shopping. Invest with that money, widen your revenue stream, make that money work for you and keep it safe to take care of you in your older years. Leave an inheritance for your loved ones so that you will never say "I wish I knew better"

13. The Good Love That Got Away:

Is there that great person in your life loving you good? Don't push that person away, or else that person will walk out your life and you will never ever find someone that incredible and who connects with you all your life. It will torment you to grow older with thoughts of "What if I was still with that person?"

14. The Parents You Despised:

When younger, it is easy to show contempt to your parents; what do your parents know? They are old-fashioned, shady and small -minded. But your parents are still your parents whether you agree with them or not, whatever their style. Don't let your parent die or get separated from you, reconcile and make up.

When you get older, you will realize why your parents wanted to be close to you. The older you get, the more you see the value.

To Realize The Value Of:

1. A sister or brother, ask someone who doesn't have one.

2. Ten years, ask a newly divorced couple.

3. Four years, ask a graduate.

4. One year, ask a student who has failed a final exam.

5. Nine months, ask a mother who gave birth to a still-born.

6. One month, ask a mother who has given birth to a premature baby.

7. One week, ask an editor of a weekly newspaper.

8. One minute, ask a person who has missed the train, bus or plane.

9.One second, ask a person who has survived an accident.

10. A friend or family member, LOSE ONE.

Thanks for reading quietly.

A REFLECTIVE EXAMPLE

During a robbery, the bank robber shouted to everyone in the bank: "Don't move. The money belongs to the state. Your life belongs to you." Everyone in the bank laid down quietly. This is called "mind changing concept" changing the conventional way of thinking.

The robber provocatively shouted at the lady on the bank counter table: "please be civilized! This is a robbery and not a rape!" This is called "being professional" focus only on what you are trained to do!

When the bank robbers returned home, the young robber (MBA-trained) told the older robber (who has only completed year 6 in primary school): "Big brother, let's count how much we got." The older rebutted and said:

"You are very stupid. There is so much money it will take us a long time to count. Tonight, the TV News will tell us how much we robbed from the bank!"

This is called "Experience." Nowadays, experience is more important than paper qualifications!

After the robbers had left, the bank manager told the bank supervisor to call the police quickly. But the supervisor said to him: "wait! Let us take out $10 million from the bank for ourselves and add it to the $7 million that we have embezzled from the bank." This is called "swim with the tide." Converting an unfavorable situation to advantage!

The supervisor says: "It will be good if there is a robbery every month." This is called "Killing boredom." Personal Happiness is more important than your job. The next day, the TV-News reported that $20 million was taken from the bank.

The robbers counted, but they could only count $3 million. The bank manager took $17 million with a snap of his fingers. It looks like it is better to be educated than to be a thief!"

This is called "Knowledge is worth as much as gold!"

The bank manager was smiling and happy because his losses in the share market are now covered by his robbery. This is called "Seizing the opportunity." Daring to the risks! So, who are the real robbers here?